2-18-15

To Joe + Faye

A Solid Couple we
Always Admire

Ray Lane

Sharecropper's Dream

ROY RAINS

and

KIMBERLY ALLISON

WESTBOW
PRESS
A DIVISION OF THOMAS NELSON
& ZONDERVAN

WestBow Press books may be ordered through booksellers or by contacting:

WestBow Press
A Division of Thomas Nelson & Zondervan
1663 Liberty Drive
Bloomington, IN 47403
www.westbowpress.com
1-(866) 928-1240

Cover photo: Joy Rains and his team, 1940.

ISBN: 978-1-4908-0003-5 (sc)
ISBN: 978-1-4908-0005-9 (hc)
ISBN: 978-1-4908-0004-2 (e)

Library of Congress Control Number: 2013911885

Printed in the United States of America.

WestBow Press rev. date: 11/06/2014

For the next generation

Table of Contents

Acknowledgments

Special Thanks to:

"Campa" and "Nanny" Rains – for living a life worth sharing

Aunt Margaret – for the other side of every story

Gary Price – for supplying valuable background information

Bill and Susan Sweeny – for formatting the pictures

Scott Price and Timothy Allison – for literally wading through the manure to get the perfect "author" shot

Hannah Grace Allison – for helping transcribe Uncle Roy's cassette tapes

Everyone who encouraged us to write the book!

Introduction

Fifteen-year-old Timothy and I were painting the porch rails when he casually mentioned, "Mom, it seems odd to me that a lot of kids don't know how to work."

"What do you mean?"

"Well, for one thing, they only work hard while the boss is watching, and for another, they want to start taking breaks before we even get started."

The answer to the dilemma was clear to me. "They didn't have your Uncle Roy teaching them to work when they were younger."

Timothy's eyes lit up. "That's it! Uncle taught us to do all kinds of work! He took us to clean out barns, fix fences, pick berries, plant potatoes...," the list went on and on. "And whatever we did, I always tried to work as hard as Uncle!"

Timothy returned to the paint bucket with a smile full of good memories while I wondered, "Who taught Uncle Roy to work?"

With a little prompting, Uncle chronicled his life story on two cassette tapes. After listening to his narrative, I realized Uncle Roy's code of conduct came from a long line of hardworking sharecroppers. "Survival" was the harsh teacher of diligence and endurance, while honest work was its own reward.

With this understanding, how can the discipline of the past be brought to bear on the present? Without cotton fields and milk pails, how will future generations ever learn a hearty work ethic? It is my hope that this collection of "Uncle Roy stories" will inspire young people to develop the character qualities that can, and did, make dreams happen. By rubbing shoulders with yesterday's sharecroppers, we can't help but stand a little taller, work a little harder, hang a little tougher.

~ *Kimberly Allison*

Prologue

Feb 16, 1998

I am sitting in my son, Cary Lee's, dining room, looking south. The first thing I see is the Old Home Place, where so many memories still live. Between here and there is nothing but black and red Limousine cattle stretched out for close to half a mile. My, how things have changed in the last fifty years. I look to my left, and I imagine cotton rows. My dad was a cotton farmer. He loved cotton. We toiled all summer to keep the weeds and grass from taking it over so we could pick it. I look to my right, and I imagine corn fields, "head feed," as we called it. We raised it for our cattle and hogs.

This was the first piece of land my dad ever owned, and he was almost forty-six years old. He had farmed all around this area in several places as a sharecropper and always gave one-third of the grain and one-fourth of the cotton to the landlord. But now, for the first time in his life, he would be able to keep everything he grew.

My parents, Joy and Ruth Rains

1

A Father's Heart

I was born August 10, 1930. I would later tease my mother by saying I must have been the most unwanted kid in the country. For one thing, she already had three children when I came along. Junior was nine, Louise was seven, and Margaret was five. For another thing, the Depression and drought had wiped out everything less than a year before I was born. People were going bankrupt and losing fortunes. It was a tough year and a tough decade. The 1930s were bleak.

My grandfather had lost his place, across the road from here, which he purchased in 1919. He still owed eight hundred dollars on eighty acres of good land, but he might as well have owed eight million dollars, because there was no way he could pay it off. My dad leased the place in 1929 from the people who repossessed it from my grandfather, and we lived there for ten years. Later, we would call it the "Old Rains Place."

My mother often told this story about the Christmas of 1930, when I was just a baby. Like I said before, times were hard. When the stock market crashed, folks couldn't sell the products they had worked so hard to raise. There just wasn't any money, and there wouldn't have been anything to eat had we not raised our own food. That's what kept us alive and healthy. We didn't have to depend on money, that way, to go and buy everything.

So in 1930, the three older children were told there would be no Christmas that year. There wouldn't even be any candy. There wouldn't be anything at all – no gifts of any kind. But they had already become accustomed to hanging their socks. They would always hang their stockings, then Christmas morning, when they would get up, there would always be something in the socks. But they had been told this was one year that they would just have to forget it.

Nevertheless, Mother said the three older children crept in, one by one, hung their socks, and went on to bed. My dad sat there, looking at those socks, and he couldn't stand it. Even though it was only about two degrees above zero outside, he took off walking two miles to the McLain store. His cousin and her husband ran the store, and they let him have some oranges, apples, and candy on credit to put in those kids' socks. Then when they got up the next morning, there was at least something there for them.

Every time Mother told that story, she could hardly keep tears from coming to her eyes, and I have the same problem every time I think about it. Daddy had walked two miles in that bitter cold weather to try to find something for those kids because they had, in good faith, hung their socks, thinking something surely would come about. And surely it did.

2

The Cattle Roundup

The drought lasted for six years, from 1930 to 1936, with 1934 being one of the worst years. It was very severe. There was no grass growing, no feed for the animals, and no hay being made, so there was no way to winter the cattle. My dad believed the cattle were going to die anyway, so he signed up on the government program to have all his cattle killed. He figured if he did that, he could at least get some return for all the work he had put into them. The program paid five dollars for yearling heifers, seven dollars and fifty cents for two-year-old heifers, and ten dollars for grown cows. My dad's whole herd brought around three hundred and seventy-five dollars.

When the government men came down to kill the cattle, I was four years old. I had been told to stay out of the way so I wouldn't get hurt. I remember standing outside the lot fence, where my dad and some of the men had penned the cattle. I watched as the government men began to shoot the cattle. A man came by wanting to take one of the cows home with him.

He said he'd be glad to give the government their ten dollars. He had a place for it, and he could take care of it. But they said no, because my dad had signed up for the cattle to be shot, and they were going to be shot.

I remember my mother, my grandmother, and my aunt got together at the Old Rains Place, where we lived at the time, and canned meat all day, on everything that could cook, until the cattle began to spoil. There was no refrigeration, so the only way to keep meat from spoiling was to can it in pressure cookers. Everyone worked as fast as they could to save as much meat as possible. My dad and the men skinned and cleaned animals as they were being shot and brought the meat into the kitchen for the ladies to can.

When it finally began to spoil, they dragged the rest of the cattle by teams of horses to the back side of the pasture under the persimmon trees. My uncle even took a wagon-load to feed his bird dogs. For years after that, whenever I wandered around the pasture, I would walk among those bones and remember the day the cattle were shot.

3

Little Milker

On November 2, 1934, my little sister, Sally, was born. Margaret and I were sent to stay with Grandma and Grandpa, about two miles north, for about a week. We did not appreciate this arrangement because they got up way before daybreak, and went to bed before dark. We were so excited to get to go back home and see the new baby. Sally was the last of the five children born into my family.

Around our house, you were never too young to help. I remember going to the cow lot early in the morning with my brother, older sisters, and dad to milk cows. Every morning, as soon as there was enough light to see, we were milking. I know I was only five years old, watching the others milk, when Margaret said, "Come over here, and see if you can milk Speck. I think you could milk her. She won't kick."

Margaret encouraged me, and I felt really proud to be able to work alongside the older kids. "That's the way! See, you can milk like a grown-up," she coaxed.

I had milk all over me, the bucket, and Margaret. It took

me as long to milk my cow as it did for the others to milk all of their cows put together. But from then on, that was my cow to milk. I wasn't even old enough to go to school, but I was determined to work as hard as the rest of the kids. It made me feel important. I eventually graduated to milking more and more of the herd, until I could milk any cow on the place. It wasn't until much later that I realized Margaret had hoodwinked me. If she could train me to milk one cow, that was one less cow for her to have to milk.

This is my little sister Sally and me in front of
the Old Rains Place where I was born.

4

An Honest Man

In 1939, when I was nine years old, we moved to the Pugh Place. This was less than a mile north from where I live today. We called it the Pugh Place because a man named Pugh owned it. He lived in Muskogee and worked at the federal courthouse. The Pugh Place had fifty more acres with it than the Old Rains Place had - one hundred thirty acres compared to eighty. I guess Daddy thought his kids were getting bigger, and they could work more land. The problem was that the new farmland was harder to work. It was good land, but it had "gumbo" soil. Gumbo was dark, sticky, and heavy, and needed more moisture than the soil we had before. Some years it made good crops, and some years it didn't.

Mr. Pugh came down twice a year. He came when the strawberries were ripe, because we had a beautiful strawberry patch. And he came when we started picking cotton, because one-fourth of the cotton, and one-third of the grain would be his. My dad would sell the cotton and give the landlord one-fourth of what the cotton brought. When we gathered the grain, we would harvest ten rows and leave five, all the way across the field. My dad would always call his landlord and tell him to come and look at the field to make sure Dad had left him his third.

I remember the landlord coming down, and I walked with Daddy and him to the field. When he finished counting the rows, he stood up straight and announced, "That's exactly the way it is supposed to be."

And if you knew my dad, you would know that's the *only* way it was going to be. I don't remember the landlord ever coming back to count the corn again. He knew my dad was an honest man and would give him what he had coming.

In 1939, there was still no electricity, and I don't know how my parents and other folks made it with no electricity. Everything, from housework to farming, was done the hard way. There were no electric washing machines and no refrigerators to keep the milk from spoiling. However, we milked two times a day, so it didn't have to keep for very long. It is amazing to me how my parents survived, raised a house full of kids, and did what they did without any modern conveniences.

5

Playing with Fire

Another chore Margaret encouraged me to get involved with was gathering wood chips. It started out to be her job, until one day she decided I was old enough to do it. She showed me how to go around where Daddy had been chopping wood with his ax, and gather up all the chips that flew from the logs. The chips would dry out, and Daddy would use them with a little kerosene to start a fire for the bigger wood. My dad would get up at about four or five in the morning, and there had better be plenty of chips to build a fire with. So my new job was to make sure there was a bucketful of chips waiting by the wood stove every evening.

One cold night, while Mama and Daddy were out, Margaret and I decided to build a fire. Daddy had only told us about a thousand times not to mess with the wood stove, so we should have been more cautious. But Margaret was the ring leader. She talked me into it.

We put the chips in the stove, threw on some kerosene, added the dry wood, and we built a fire. I mean, we built a *fire*.

It got hotter and hotter. The wall was so hot you couldn't even put your hand on it. This particular house had eight to nine rolls of wallpaper on it to keep the wind out. We knew very well all of that paper could go up in flames. We began to panic and try to shut the stove down, but the way they built them in those days, it was hard to control them. We really couldn't shut it down.

We ran outside and saw the tar around the chimney and on the roof was melting. We could smell it. I guess if the house would have burned, I wouldn't be here today. My dad would have killed us both. I think we came as close to burning it down as you could get, without it actually catching fire. That was probably the most terrified I have ever been in my whole life. I look back on that fire, and I am amazed the house didn't burn down. I hope Margaret learned her lesson.

6

The Hen House

We had a neighbor to the north of us named Luther Crawford. One day, when I was nine years old, he walked over to where I was working with Daddy and asked me if I would clean out his chicken house. He didn't say anything about what he was going to pay me to do it, but I thought maybe he would give me a dime. I said, "Sure, I'll clean it out."

I was excited to get the chance to possibly earn some pocket money. As soon as Daddy let me go, I headed over to Luther's hen house and got busy with a shovel and rake. I shoveled the chicken litter into buckets, carried them to Luther's garden, and dumped them. I could only carry one bucketful at a time. I can't tell you how many buckets and trips it took me to get it all cleaned out. Every now and then, it would cross my mind, "I hope he gives me a dime."

The hen house was about ten by fifteen feet, and I guess it took me half a day to clean it out. I kept going until every crumb was shoveled out of there. When I finally got the last bucket dumped, I found Luther and told him I was finished. I was still hoping he would give me a dime. I stood and waited while he looked the chicken house over. I watched him reach in his pocket and pull out a fifty cent piece and give it to me!

To my knowledge, that was the first work I had ever gotten paid to do. I was not only surprised, but very excited that he thought that much of my work. I took it home and showed it to my folks. I kept thinking he must have really been pleased with my work to have given me a fifty cent piece. I thought I must have done a good job.

That encouraged me even more to work hard and be thorough with every job I had. That's true whether you work on the farm or "work out" somewhere else. The discipline is the same. When you are assigned to do something, give it all you've got.

Luther had one son named Luther, Jr. We called him Little Tar. If it rained, Little Tar would be over to visit because he knew we were rained out of field work. Or, he would come over at dark, because he knew we quit at dark. Little Tar bounced around from our house to the Cole's, to the Scoggins' that lived just up the road, to the Scott's. We enjoyed Little Tar slipping off to our house, because his dad would act like he had lost him and had to hunt for him, but he always knew where Little Tar was. It was a good time of life.

We met some good people when we moved to the Pugh Place. The Cole family, with their grandchildren, Jerry and Evelyn, became good friends. Even today, we still see each other about once a year. They were honest, hardworking, beautiful people; among the finest that I have ever met.

*Miss Lemmons and my 5th grade class. I'm in the
middle of the front row with a baseball glove.*

7

Teacher's Pet

My brother, Joy "Junior," was nine years older than me, and in 1939, when he was 18, Junior joined the CCC. There wasn't much work available for the young people, other than farming, so the government came up with a program called the Civilian Conservation Corp. Junior left home and went to Skull Creek, Colorado. I will never forget the letters we got from Skull Creek. As a child, I envisioned a creek with skulls running down it. That's a kid for you. But I remember Junior was always an idol to me. He had a lot of influence on me as a youngster, and even as an adult, right up till the time he passed away. He influenced what I did, where I went, and how I behaved myself.

At that time, we attended school in McLain. It was a native rock schoolhouse, built by the CCC. There were two rooms and two teachers in the school. The "little room" was for kids in first through fourth grade, and the "big room" was for kids in fifth through eighth grade. There were about forty kids in each room.

We started every day with the flag salute. Then, every Friday afternoon, to break up the schoolwork, we had a "ciphering" contest. Two kids would go up to the black board, and the teacher would call out a long math problem. Whoever worked it out first would stay up there. The loser would go sit down, and another would take his place.

One of my fondest memories of school was a beautiful young lady named Edna Lemmons who came to teach in the big room of McLain School. This teacher would have a great influence on my life. Her kindness and concern made her not only *my* favorite teacher, but the favorite of just about every kid in both rooms, as well. Miss Lemmons gave the impression that she enjoyed kids and enjoyed teaching by making every student feel special. Her beauty and charm seemed like a breath of fresh air in a dark world. Miss Lemmons taught all four of my years in the big room and then taught another year and a half after I graduated from eighth grade. She was single at the time but married a soldier toward the end of WWII.

I had the pleasure of contacting Miss Lemmons in 1978, and we corresponded several times after that. She passed away a few months ago, and I attended her funeral. I was honored to meet her two daughters and say a few words on her behalf. Her daughters later accused me of having a schoolboy crush on their mother. Maybe they were right.

8

The Big Apple

When I was in the third grade, I would walk to school with my sisters, Margaret and Sally. At that time, Sally was probably five years old, and Margaret was around thirteen. It was a mile and a half to the McLain School, so if we left home by 8:00, we usually made it to school in good time for the 8:30 bell.

One day, we learned the government would be bringing some apples and oranges in a wagon for the children to eat at school. When my dad found out, he gave us strict orders not to touch the fruit on that wagon. Case closed.

When we arrived at the school yard the next day, there was the wagon loaded with fruit. Up on top of the pile was one of the biggest apples I had ever seen in my life. We had to walk right past that wagon to get into the school building. My sisters and I never even entertained the thought of taking a piece of fruit.

With Daddy, there was no grey area or "middle ground." It was all "Daddy's ground." He didn't allow any begging when his mind was made up. And I don't remember a time when it wasn't. The answer was either yes or no.

There were other kids besides us who did not eat the apples, but not many. They did not eat because they were forbidden, just like we were. The kids who *did* get to eat the fruit tried to entice us to eat, too. They even teased us a little. But it didn't work. When Daddy said. "No," he meant it. If we disobeyed, we knew we'd regret it later.

All day, from my desk, I could see the apple wagon with that huge apple on top of the pile. I could see it through the window while I did my arithmetic, spelling, grammar, and history. I walked past it to go to recess and lunch. I wanted that apple on the top more than I have wanted any apple before or since, mainly because it was so big.

However, there was no debate in my mind that maybe Daddy wouldn't find out, because it was settled. I really tried not to think about the apple too much. We walked home that afternoon, and I still wanted that apple. But I didn't get it.

When we got home, neither of my parents even asked us if we had eaten any of the fruit. They had trained us to obey and show self-control, but there was a deeper principle here. They had also trained us to work for what we had. Maybe there was a certain amount of pride involved, in a good sense. Daddy was glad to be able to work to provide for his family. And as long as he was able, he really didn't want any help.

9

Room to Spare

ince ninety percent of the folks that lived around us were sharecroppers, we were all in about the same boat, financially. No one felt any poorer or richer than anyone else. 'Most every house around us had a bed in the living room. That was for the parents. There would usually be one bedroom for the kids. The baby would generally sleep with the parents in the front room, because the wood stove was there, and it was warmer. At the Pugh Place, we also had a small room tacked onto the back of the house. That was where Ralph, the school bus driver, stayed.

Ralph lived in Oktaha, where the school was located. Every evening, when he drove the kids home from school, he would finish up at our house and just stay overnight. Then, the next morning, he would start out from our house and pick up the kids as he headed back to Oktaha. That way, he would not have to make the long fifteen-mile drive back and forth.

In the winter, the add-on room got so cold, that before morning, Ralph would usually be in bed with Junior and me.

We boys shared a bed, and the girls shared a bed in the same room. No one thought anything about it at the time. In the mornings, Ralph would get up early and go outside so everyone could get ready with some privacy. He never ate breakfast with us, although mama would always ask. He didn't want to impose any more than he thought he already was.

Ralph wasn't the only bus driver who stayed with us. Before him, it was Mr. Merrifield, at the Old Rains Place, where I was born. Later on, there were others who needed a place to stay, for whatever reason, and they were always welcome at our house. Strangers were treated like family, and we always had food to share. Hospitality was just a way of life.

My school picture when I was 6 years old.

10

What's In a Name?

We didn't have any alarm clocks to wake us up in the morning, but we didn't really operate by the clock, anyway. We just went to bed at dark, and got up at dawn. When it was time to get up, Daddy would stand at my door and say, "Clabe."

I would jump out of bed, slip on my coveralls, and take off. There was no whining and begging to stay in bed, and no pretending you didn't hear him. We had work to do, and we needed to get started.

No one knew why Daddy called me "Clabe," nor why he called any of the other kids the nicknames he gave them, but we had them from the time we were born. I don't remember my Dad ever calling me "Roy." I was "Clayburn" to him, but he would use "Clay" or "Clabe" for short. He called Junior "Happy Jack," or just "Hap." Margaret was "Barchie," Sally was nicknamed "Cutto," and we called Louise "Artie." The boys' nicknames really stuck, and most of the old timers from around here still call me Clayburn.

Besides having a nickname, we all thought we had a middle name while we were growing up. We found out later there were no middle names on our birth certificates. When I registered with the Navy, I signed in as Roy George Rains. A little later, the officer informed me that my name was not Roy George. He said if I wanted to, I could put George on the form, anyway. I told him to put George. But, later, I wished I had told him to put Clay, since I had the choice. So, while I was in the Navy, my name was Roy George. But after I got out, I started putting Roy Clay on my documents. You would think this would have caused some legal problems later on, but so far, it hasn't.

11

World War II

In 1939 and 1940, war clouds were looming on the horizon, and things looked rough. Many people didn't believe that there would ever be another world war, but in 1939, it didn't look good. Germany was taking over smaller countries. Japan was rattling its swords and had jumped onto some of the Chinese territories, including Manchuria and others. It was beginning to be a troubled time in the world. We got little news where we lived, since we had no T.V., satellite, internet, or computers.

December 7, 1941, the Japanese bombed Pearl Harbor and brought us into WWII. Germany, Japan, and Italy were on the Axis side, and the United States, Great Britain, and other countries were on the Allies side. Nearly all the men from eighteen to forty years old were showing their loyalty to the country in some form of service.

WWII changed the face of America forever. The boys that went to war had never been away from home, and they came back different. They had seen something besides cotton patches, cornfields, and hog killings. Life would never be the same for them.

When WWII started, my older brother, Junior, was caught up in it. About six months into the war, he, along with my favorite cousin, Raymond, enlisted in the United States Navy. They left in June of 1942 to go into the service. We would not see them again (except for two short leaves) until the last part of 1945, when the war was over and they were discharged.

My oldest sister, Louise, married in 1941 and moved off to California. That put all the farm work on Margaret and me, since Sally wasn't old enough to help much.

Gary, my parent's first grandchild, was born to Louise the year after she got married. Since he was born in 1942, when everything began to change, he would have no understanding of the way of life we had before the war. America changed so much then. But the 1940s were good years, even in spite of the war.

Old Bat

12

Old Bat

In the early 1940s, all the farm work was done by horses, but we normally didn't raise our own horses. We bought them from the neighbors or at the sale. When I was eleven years old, in 1941, there was a horse born on a farm up the road from us. We could see it as we walked to school and back, and I thought it sure was a pretty foal. He had a white spot on his side that looked like a flying bat, so they named him Bat. He also had a white blaze down the front of his face and some white on his legs. Every time I saw him, I thought about how much I would love to have that horse.

I would go over to the neighbor's place whenever I could and check on the foal. I would pet it and talk to it for a few minutes before I had to run back home and get busy with chores. From our house, I would sometimes see it tied to another older horse in their pasture. That's how they broke it to ride. Bat was never broke to work in the field, since he was foaled from a riding horse.

For three years, I watched Bat grow up. I knew I would

never be able to buy him or even get a ride on him. None of my older siblings had owned a riding horse, and it was foolish to think about owning one myself, although I always wished I could.

My brother, Junior, came home on leave from the Navy in 1944, when I was fourteen. We were all excited to see him and wanted to tell him everything that had happened while he was gone. I wanted to show him the horse I thought was so beautiful. I told him that Bat would no doubt be a fine riding horse, since the mare was such a good, fast horse.

A few days later, Junior said, "I think I'll buy that horse over there, if you will take care of him for me." Words can't describe what I felt at that moment. I couldn't believe this extraordinary animal was going to be mine! Junior may have thought it was really his, but to me, it was really mine!

Junior bought the horse for sixty-five dollars and gave it to me. In thirty horses, Bat stood out among the herd. He was faster than any of my friends' horses. He would do anything I told him to do and would go wherever I pointed him. I taught him to jump the gate to the pasture, so I wouldn't have to get off and open it. First, I would walk him up to the gate, back him off, and then . . . away we'd go, over the gate!

Bat was not afraid of anything, and he loved to swim. Sometimes, on Sunday afternoons, we would ride our horses to the Arkansas River and try to cross it on horseback. It was no fun to cross unless it was up at about flood level, with logs floating past and the water swirling. When I crossed it on Bat, I would usually drift about a quarter-mile downstream, so I started walking Bat a quarter-mile upstream first, then we would cross.

I have so many happy memories of that horse. He was the greatest horse in this part of the country. Bat stayed with our family for twenty-three years. It was a major highlight of my life to own and have a relationship with this kind of animal, and it would never have been possible if it hadn't been for my brother's generosity.

This is some of my buddies and me (2nd from left) getting ready to go riding in 1946.

13

Good Friends

We stayed out of the field on Sundays, unless it was a dire emergency. We would have to do chores like milk the cows, bring in wood, and such like, but no field work. It seemed everybody around here took Sundays off, even though they didn't go to church much.

The closest church was Elm Grove, a little over two miles away, and sometimes, my buddies and I would ride our horses over there. There was a big concrete cellar outside the church, and we would stay out there on our horses and listen to the singing and preaching through the open windows.

On Sunday afternoons, there was always a fried chicken dinner at Granny Rains's house, then we'd go fishing, squirrel hunting, or visiting with the neighbors. We had a special bond with the neighbors because we all had about the same life experiences and goals. We had some good fellowship with some good friends.

Walter and Mattie Coppin and their four sons were in this area since the late thirties. In 1937, they bought the Old

Rains Place, where I was born, and moved there a year later. We became good friends with them and their children. I was buddies with all of them; however, Marvin was probably the best friend I ever had. When Marvin married Anna, they made a dollar apiece for a full day's work chopping corn. On top of that, they had to walk three miles to get to the corn field! That was a hard-earned dollar!

Charlie and Bonnie Nail moved into the community a little later on, when I was about five or six years old. In 1937, they rented the Old Home Place, where we eventually lived. We became the best of friends, and one of my closest friends was their oldest son, Charlie, Jr.

The Fuller family lived east of us for years. "Coonie" was a little older than me, but he and his wife, Duby, were our good friends, along with their children, Jerry, C.A., and Bryce.

I'm sure I will miss some of the families in the community, but there were the Chessers, Scoggins, Webbs, Holders, and Nipps families. They were all good friends. Sissy Gaither was a fine man we always had fun with, and I enjoyed working with him.

Barrel, Ted, and Dink Scott, Bill Jones, and the Roberts family were all good neighbors. We helped them gather their crops down in the bottom and actually got paid for it. At home, there was no cash flow, but when we worked out for others, we got paid.

14

The Great Flood

The greatest flood ever recorded in Oklahoma's history hit the Arkansas River in 1943. It had rained for several days and water had backed up behind the Pensacola Dam. The Corp of Engineers wouldn't release any of the water out of the dam, thinking it would quit raining, but it didn't. When they finally let the water go, it flooded the Arkansas River downstream.

It took about ten days for the flood to reach us, since we lived five miles from the river. There were five families that we knew of who lived pretty close to the river whose houses were washed completely away. Some of the families tied their houses down, when they realized the flood was coming. They used ropes and tied on to the trees around there.

We could stand on a bluff by our house and see all across the area that the flood water covered. We watched it get deeper and closer. From where we stood, we could see the roof-tops of the houses that had been tied down. We were mainly keeping watch to see if we would be trapped on our property with no way out. Mama and Daddy had started packing up some things just in case we had to leave in a hurry.

As the water got closer to our house, we would put a stake in the ground at the water's edge, to mark the water level. Then, I'd race every morning to be the first to see how much higher it had gotten during the night. It took about ten days to reach its highest peak, which was just under our back doorstep. It looked like an ocean.

The adults were concerned, but since I was just a kid, I thought it was fun. My dad would pace the floor, worried about the crop. It flooded in May, so we had already planted the fields. Every day, as the water rose, it would wash out a little more of the crop. It took about ten to twenty days for the water to run back down after it peaked. When the ground dried out enough, we started all over. We plowed, cultivated, and re-planted. It cost more, and the crop came in late that year, but we did it. We had to. It was our living, and when your livelihood depends on the weather, you have to be flexible.

My dad lived there five years, and in 1944, we moved to the Spain Place.

15

Quail Dinner

Lucille Spain, another school teacher in our community, taught in McLain School. She was a great teacher and a beautiful person. She and her husband were friends of ours. Her husband was in the Army, and had been captured by the Germans. When she found this out, she had a nervous breakdown. She asked my dad if he would come over and take care of her place until they found out what became of Mr. Spain.

Dad didn't really want to move over there, but he agreed to, just to help her out. The Spain Place was east of us about two miles. We lived there two years, until we moved to the place we are today, the place my dad bought, which we now call the Home Place.

The Spain Place had a good mountain to hunt and good creeks to fish. We had neighbors named Aunt Nettie Marshall and her nephew, Charlie Ray. He and I hunted together, and had some good times over there.

I remember Thanksgiving 1944, when I was fourteen years

old. We had just moved to the Spain place. On Thanksgiving Day, Chap Bartleson, a friend of my dad's, came down to bird hunt with him. My dad was a good squirrel hunter, but he was also pretty good at hunting quail. Chap owned a hardware store in town, and he was rich. He had two really pretty bird dogs that he brought with him. I wanted to go hunting with them, but they didn't want me to. They went east of the Spain place, and hunted toward Aunt Nettie Marshall's place. There was always quail in there. My dad knew exactly where they were.

I went west toward Ted Scott's place. I only had a single barrel twenty-guage I had borrowed from Uncle John Herriman. It belonged to my cousin, Tobe, but he was in the Army, so they let me use it while he was gone. I found some quail about a quarter mile west of our house. I knew a covey of quail lived there, because I had watched them raise their broods there. I killed six and brought them in at about 10:00 that morning. Mother said, "If you will clean those, I will fix them for Thanksgiving dinner."

Mother made a nice dinner with my quail. About dinner time, Dad and Mr. Bartleson came in from hunting. They had not even fired a shot, much less seen a quail. My mother invited Mr. Bartleson to eat dinner with us, and he said he would. He agreed to eat with us because he wasn't through hunting for the day. They sat down to my quail and my mom's cooking. We had everything off the land – homemade biscuits, potatoes, gravy, and homemade pie.

I'll never forget what happened after the meal. Mr. Bartleson, one of the richest men in Muskogee, stood up and said to my mother, "Mrs. Rains, that is the finest Thanksgiving Dinner that I have ever eaten."

When he said that, I felt really excited because I figured he was telling the truth. I knew he could have afforded anything he wanted to eat, and had probably eaten at many fancy restaurants I thought, "I am only fourteen years old, and I have impressed one of the richest men in town with my quail!"

That started a tradition with me. I determined that every Thanksgiving dinner from then on, I would make sure mama had something to cook that I had shot. I missed a few of those years when I was in the service, but otherwise, I always tried to bring in wildlife from the land for Thanksgiving Day. And it all started with those six quail in 1944.

*My 8th grade class with Miss Lemmons in
the center and me on the far right.*

16

Cotton Pickin' School

*W*hen I was a kid, McLain School didn't start until just after Labor Day. We would have school for about a month, then they would shut down the school so the kids could help their families pick cotton. The choice was either close down or count everyone absent. There was no set schedule for when the school would close. It all depended on the weather and the crops. After thirty to forty-five days of picking, we would be back in school. The second picking didn't seem to get as much consideration from the school. It was more or less every man for himself.

There was one fella who didn't get to come to school very often at all. His dad did things a little differently from the other farmers around here. He was a trapper. After the crops were in, he would start trapping, and he wanted his son to help him with the traps and the animals they caught. So, this boy could only go to school every now and then. He finally graduated from the eighth grade when he was eighteen years old. I admired him for that. He stayed with it.

Webbers Falls High School didn't operate like McLain. They had a system where the local farmers would come to the school at 1:00 to pick up any kids who wanted to work cotton. Then, they would bring them back in time to catch the school bus home at 3:30. The only requirement was you had to bring your own cotton sack. I took mine with me, folded it up, and sat on it while I rode the bus back and forth to school. Daddy didn't mind me being available for the other farmers, so long as I was available for him when I got home!

17
From Daylight to Dark

In 1944, I started my first year of high school at Webbers
Falls School. Sally was still in school at McLain, and
she had to walk two and a half miles every morning to
school, and two and a half miles back home. I walked a half
mile down to the main road to catch a school bus to Webbers
Falls.

I know this is going to be hard for you youngsters to
understand or even believe, but every morning, before I went
to school, Margaret and I would get up way before daylight (in
the wintertime, especially) and we would milk about twenty-
five cows by hand. Then we would separate the milk from
the cream and take care of all of that business. This was all
done before I would walk down to catch the school bus. Every
evening, when I would come in, we'd milk all those cows
again.

Daddy never had to tell me to be home in time to milk.
It was my responsibility, and we had an understanding that I
would be there at the right time every day. The cows had to

be milked before dark. Then the next morning, we'd get up and start all over again!

This went on for the biggest part of 1944 into 1945. When school was almost out for the summer, I convinced my mother and dad there was no other way for us to get along than for me to quit school. I claimed it was just too hard on them, and I acted like it was too hard on me. I realize now it really wasn't. I could have gotten an education if I had really wanted to. But I would much rather work than sit in school. So, I coaxed them, talked to them, and hounded them, and finally, they let me quit.

Junior was in the service, and Margaret, in the meantime, had married and moved off. So, finally it was just Dad and me doing the milking and all the other chores. We worked together the rest of the time we stayed on the Spain Place.

In 1944 through 1945, the war was winding down. I remember I was a half mile east of our house on a bluff hunting squirrel, when I heard a shotgun go off. My dad had gone out in the yard and shot his double-barreled shot gun, because word had come on the battery-powered radio that the Germans had surrendered. WWII was just about over.

The war with Germany was over in May 1945, and Japan surrendered in August. That same year, Junior came home just before Christmas. We were all together. 1945 was the best Christmas in a long time for us.

18
Fenced In

My dad had bought the Home Place earlier in the year of 1945, but could not get possession of it until Jan 1, 1946. So we stayed on the Spain place until we could move in. Forrest Spain was released from the German prison camp where he almost died. We were so thankful he came home. He was as skinny as a broom handle, but he was alive. They were getting ready to move back to their place as we prepared to move to the Home Place.

The Home Place was pretty run down, and it needed work. It had been rented out many times, sometimes for cash rent, sometimes for crop rent, and the previous owners had let it run down. So, before we could move in, we had to rebuild all the fences.

We cut the fence posts for it at Aunt Nettie's place in August of 1945 when it was about one hundred degrees. It took nearly the whole month of August to make enough fence posts. Dad, Charlie Ray Weaver, and I did the work. Charlie helped us make the posts, and in return, he and Aunt Nettie got to keep the tops out of the trees for firewood.

We used Post-Oak trees because they made the best fence posts. That is probably how they got their name. They were different than other oak trees, because they would split all the way down, unless they had two or three limbs, which made it hard to get past the knots. These posts would last about twelve years in the ground. Daddy wouldn't cut down the small trees. We had to split the bigger trees because Daddy said they would last longer if they were split. We could split four to six fence posts from a six foot length of tree trunk.

We split them with an ax and wooden wedges which we made ourselves. The wedges would last for maybe one tree, and then we would have to make more. We had one metal chisel we used to split the tree down just far enough to get a wooden wedge in there. Then, we would split it the rest of the way with the wooden wedge.

I wouldn't say it was fun to cut and split six hundred fence posts in one hundred degree weather among the ticks, flies and snakes, but we didn't slow down. Daddy was known for his diligence. We brought the fence posts up here to the Home Place and had enough to keep our cattle in. Junior was living with us at the time and helped us move.

*The five of us kids, from left to right: Sally,
Junior, Louise, me, and Margaret.*

19

Hog Killin'

We had a big hog killing at Aunt Nettie Marshall's place between Christmas and New Year's Day. Dad didn't want to move the hogs alive, so we just killed them, with my brother's help, at Aunt Nettie's while it was cold and there was no danger of the meat spoiling. She had a good place to kill hogs. She had a big bathtub-like thing to put them down in and scald them.

I have nieces and nephews pushing fifty years old that have never been to a hog killing. Hopefully, we can arrange it so that they can be in on one someday. Until then, I'm going to try to describe what we went through when we killed hogs back in the old days. This may sound gruesome to you kids, but it really isn't, because this is what they were raised for.

We would shoot the hog, and then we would cut its jugular, to get the blood out of the meat, just like they do today. Then we would put the hog in scalding hot water to get all the hair off the hide. We didn't skin hogs back then.

We left the hide on them to protect the meat when we put it in the smoke houses.

After we scraped all of the hair off, we would hang it up on a limb. Then, we would gut it and take all of its innards out. We'd strip all the fat off of the innards. Most of the time, that job went to the girls in the family.

Next, we would lay the hog down on a table, and start cutting him up. We would quarter him out, and we would have the hams, which were the hind legs. The shoulders were the front legs. We would have the sides, which made the bacon. Down the back would be the tenderloins which were the finest cuts of meat on the animal.

Then, when all of the pieces were cut, we would put a lot of salt on it, and put it in what we called a smoke house. A lot of times we would put some hickory in there and build a hickory smoke fire (It was mostly just smoke. There wasn't much fire to it.). That was to give it a flavor. You could taste the hickory flavor all the way through the winter when we would cut into that meat and eat it. We would eat on the hog all winter long and even into the summer because once it cured out, it would not spoil. If we got all the water and everything out of it, the cold weather at night would take care of it.

Then we would grind the sausage. A lot of the meat was ground up into sausage. Nothing was wasted. Last of all, we would render the lard. We would cut up the extra fat pieces into chunks and put it in a vat with a fire underneath. Then we would cook all of the lard out of it. That is what we used for grease. Your moms use Crisco and cooking oils, now. You can't buy any hog lard anymore, but back when I was a youngster, we lived on it. We would always put up enough of that lard to do us from one hog killing to the next. It would last us all year.

This is just how things were handled back in those days. This is how we had our meat. And I'm going to tell you something. That is the finest eating you can get. It might not have been good for you (They claim it wasn't. The smart people would later attest that there was too much fat in it to be really healthy.), but it tasted beautiful. It was really good.

20

Hard Work and Promises

By the time we actually moved to the Old Home Place, in January, 1946, it was two degrees above zero. It took two trips in our wagon for the furniture. The next day, we moved our cattle by horseback.

Dad and I worked together farming here at the Home Place until 1949. Farming was always hard work, and we had to do it all the hard way. Our equipment consisted of a good team of two horses, sometimes three. We had a wagon and a riding cultivator. What I mean by "riding" cultivator is it had a seat you could sit on while the horse pulled it, and it would plow one row at a time. We had a planter that planted one row at a time. We had a stalk-cutter that cut one row at a time. We had a two-sectioned harrow (we called it a "herra") that was ten feet wide and a breaking plow that would turn over twelve inches of dirt as you walked behind the team. Then we had a lister that would go down and pile the dirt both ways. It would make a ridge up there to plant stuff on top. These were the farming tools that we had at that particular time.

I never did mind the farm work, myself, but there was one thing I hated about it. I hated to see my mother having to work so hard. She always seemed too small and frail to me. One day, when I noticed her toiling along with the rest of us, I made myself a promise. I told myself that as soon as I could earn the money, I would do what I could to make her life easier.

I was twenty years old before I could make good on my promise, but I was finally able to buy mama a propane tank and a propane cook stove. Then, I saved up and bought her a refrigerator. We thought we were in tall cotton, after all those years of using an ice-box and a wood stove!

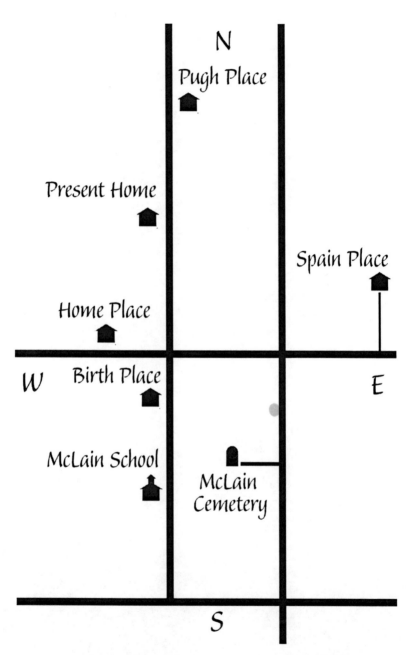

N

Pugh Place

Present Home

Spain Place

Home Place

W   Birth Place   E

McLain School

McLain
Cemetery

S

This is a map of the places we lived while I was growing up. All my life, I have lived within a range of about 2 ½ miles!

21

Kids in the Cotton Patch

After the cotton started growing, we had to "chop" it. This means we would weed it with a hoe. Then, by the 4th of July, we would "lay it by." To do this, we would plow between the rows with a cultivator, then drag the loose dirt up around the cotton plants with a hoe to choke out a little more of the weeds. Since we planted thirty to forty acres with cotton, this would take some time.

After that, in the middle of the summer, we could leave the cotton fields for a while and move over to the hay field. We would cut the hay with a team-drawn mowing machine, which cut a four foot path, then rake it into rows with a team-drawn rake. Eventually, we threw it with a pitchfork into the baling machine, called a foot-feed baler. My dad or a neighbor would jump into the baler to pack down the hay, and then jump out very quickly before he got baled right along with the hay. None of us kids were allowed to do that job because Daddy thought it was too dangerous. However, in all my years of baling hay,

I never heard of one person getting even so much as a scratch from jumping in the baler.

With the hay taken care of, it was back to the cotton fields. In the fall, when it was time to pick cotton, we big kids would each go to work with a nine-foot-long cotton sack strapped over our shoulder. The kids who were younger would get a seven-foot sack, on down to a five-foot sack for the smaller ones. The kids who were too little to drag a sack would walk along and pick the cotton that was lower to the ground and pile it in the middle of the row for us to pick up.

Remember, there were no babysitters, and no such thing as daycare. They had to take the little ones to the field in order to watch them, so why not give them something to keep them busy? They learned endurance early because they couldn't go back to the house by themselves.

22

New Shoes

We had a water bucket at one end of the cotton patch where we started, so we had to go all the way down the row and back again to get a drink. On really hot days, it seemed like forever between drinks. And then, if the bucket was empty, somebody had to take it back to the house to fill it up again.

Picking cotton, with or without water, was hard work. A nine-foot cotton sack would hold about sixty-five pounds of cotton when it was full. Three full cotton sacks was a good day's work. It would take two or three weeks to pick all of the cotton, and then we would wait a week and go over it again.

I remember one miserable day in the field complaining to my dad, "Daddy, my backbone hurts!"

He called back to me, "Son, you don't even have a backbone till you're forty!" In other words, keep working!

We kids got no wages, or even an allowance for all of the planting, hoeing, weeding, feeding, or milking, but we could count on getting paid when the cotton was harvested. Daddy would pay us for picking cotton just the same as he would pay anyone outside of the family. When it was sold, cotton would bring eight cents per pound, and we were paid two cents per pound to pick it. I could make three or four dollars on a good day of picking. That was my two cent's worth.

The only catch was at least some, if not all, of the money had to be used to buy our clothes and shoes for school. The shoes we bought were Daddy's choice. He was very picky about our shoes. Since we walked so much, and he didn't want our shoes to hurt our feet, he would take us to be fitted for shoes. Then, we would have to help pay for them. This didn't seem odd or unfair at all to me at the time. I figured I would be the one wearing the shoes, so I ought to at least pitch in for them.

After the shoes were bought, there wasn't much spending money left. But if I had enough to buy my shotgun shells and a little candy, I was happy. It was just easier to be content in those days. When you think about it, there weren't very many things that we really needed, anyway.

23

Changes

We were getting ready to put in our first crop at the Home Place, and the winds of change were already blowing. I was not quite sixteen and didn't notice at first. We got the crop planted, got it up, and were working it, when Junior decided he was going to move to Tulsa and go to work at the White Sewing Machine Company. He did exactly that and got married to a local girl named Ora Lee Brock. We had known her family for years. That left Dad, Mom, Sally, and me on the farm.

Dad had given Junior a patch of cotton to claim as his own, which he had already put a lot of work into. He had already chopped it at least once. As the owner of the ten-acre patch, Junior would get the eight cents per pound the cotton would bring in the fall, and pay his cotton pickers out of that. When I took over his patch, Junior and I made a deal to split the profits after the others had been paid their two cents per pound for picking. That was the last year Junior had anything to do with cotton patches.

Tractors were showing up, and farms were getting bigger. People could do a lot more with a tractor than with a team. Although Dad would hang on for a couple more years before he would accept the changes, it was inevitable that changes would be made in the near future. Come what may, I always thought I would grow up, marry a pretty little girl, find a piece of land, and farm it all my life, just like my dad. It was the only life I knew. Little did I realize I would be making some major changes in my life, as well, in the next few years.

24

All in a Day's Work

The next few years, we farmed at the Home Place and worked out for others, when we could, to make a little extra money. We bailed hay, and I got involved in threshing oats. Sissy Gaither had an oat thresher and threshed oats for everyone in this part of the country. One day, when I was about sixteen years old, I asked him if I could get a job threshing oats. He looked me over and said, "I'll give you a try."

So I started throwing bundles of oats onto a wagon. The guy on the wagon would stack them, haul them over to the thresher, and throw them in. He made one dollar per hour for his team and wagon, and I made only fifty cents an hour. I went home and talked Dad out of his team, then went back and told Sissy, "I'll bring you another team if you need another bundle wagon."

He said he did, and he let me do it. So, from then on, for about a month out of every summer, I would always run a bundle wagon at threshing time. Just by using a little creativity and initiative, I was able to double my income!

In 1949, I eased on up to Muskogee myself and got a job at Roselawn Dairy where my brother-in-law worked. Since I didn't have any way of getting back and forth, I moved in with him and my sister, Margaret, so I could walk to work from their house. I stayed for nearly a year with her. That was basically the end of my farming, as far as row cropping. After a couple of paychecks at Roselawn, making 75 cents an hour, I decided this city job was better than trying to beat it out with a hoe on the farm.

My dad was on his own, then, with his team of two or three horses and his one row plow. Uncle Buck had a tractor, and Dad would use it when Uncle Buck didn't need it. That helped a lot. Sally helped some, and my nephew, Gary, was old enough to be a little help.

In 1950, at nineteen years of age, I bought my first car and moved back in with Mom and Dad while I worked at the dairy. I was able to help Dad a little bit before and after work, and on my days off, but he did most of it by himself.

My parents posing with me, 1951.

25

Korean War

In the years of 1949 and 1950, another war was brewing in Korea. This would change the lives of a lot of people, just like the previous war had done. In June of 1950, war broke out between North and South Korea. The US took the side of South Korea. China, Russia, and that bunch all took the side of North Korea. The stage was set for another war, but a different kind of war than World War Two. It was the first time our nation was involved in a police action. It was fought not to win it, but to contain it right where it was, and that's what happened. Eventually, three or four years later, it ended right where it started - at the 38th parallel in Korea.

In 1950, when the Korean War started, I checked with the draft board. They said I would be called in April of 1951. Rather than wait to be drafted into the Army, I quit my job, and, along with three other boys, Donald Webb, Darrell Webb, and Jerry Cole, I decided to enlist in the Navy. It was January 2, 1951. We went to Oklahoma City and got our physicals. Three of us went on from Oklahoma City and ended up in

Chicago, in a town called Waukegan. That was where we had our boot camp.

The boot camp was right on the banks of Lake Michigan. It was snowing when we got there and snowing when we left. It snowed every day, and the wind blew every day for the entire three months of boot camp. We would have to get up between three and four in the morning to sweep the snow off the sidewalks. This was so the officers wouldn't have to walk in it. At least, that's what we figured.

If there's one thing you learn in the military, it's punctuality. By the time we finished sweeping, we had to fall in for reveille at 6:00. I was used to getting up early to milk the cows, but not at three or four in the morning! When bedtime rolled around, we had no trouble falling asleep.

25

The Plane Ride

From Waukegan, I was sent to Corpus Christie Naval Air Field. When I signed up with the Navy, I had no idea there was an air force in that branch. I thought it was all ships and water. I would never have chosen to work around airplanes, but I was assigned to the fire-fighting unit of the crash crew. We had to sit on the runway all day or all night, depending on the shift, just in case they had a crash.

I was in Corpus about one year when they put a new commander over our unit, and he wanted everybody to get to go up for a ride in the trainer plane. He started down the list alphabetically. I began to worry. I had never been up in an airplane, but I hated them. What was I going to do? I got more nervous every day as my name got closer to the top. How could I persuade him to excuse me from the plane ride?

Finally, my turn came. I went up to the commander and said, "Sir, I have never disobeyed an officer since I've been in the Navy (and I was telling the truth). Is it mandatory to ride in the plane?"

He looked at me a little puzzled and said, "No, it isn't mandatory."

"Sir, I don't want to go up."

He seemed surprised and asked, "Then, what are you doing down here?"

"Sir, my orders sent me here. I didn't ask to be here, and I've wanted to leave ever since the day I got here."

He replied, "I'll see what I can do about that." He wasn't mad. I guess he just wanted to help me out.

Three weeks later, he handed me a brown envelope with orders to be sent to Boston. I said, "Thank you, Sir!" I was so glad to be out of there.

This is my Navy dress uniform.

26

Sailing the Sea

It was the Korean War, but I never saw Korea. I was sent out from Boston on a destroyer with the Sixth Fleet, to the Mediterranean, around the Suez Canal. The Egyptian leader threatened to close the Suez Canal, but there was no action there until after I left the Navy.

When I first went out on the ship, I had the port side (left side) watch from 4:00 a.m. to 8:00 a.m. I was supposed to patrol the port side, but I barely had enough room to turn around in my tracks. My orders were to report any activity, but there was none to report. It was a long four hours.

We were in the Atlantic Ocean, and the sun came up on my side. It started out bright red, and when the sun shines on the ocean, it is extremely bright. I wore a head radio set on my ears, and one morning, for some crazy reason, I pushed my button and said, "Bright light bearing port side forty degrees."

That got the officer of the day excited. He came running up on deck to find out what "bright light" I was talking about. When he found out it was the sun, he was not amused. For my lack of respect, I had to clean something big (like the deck) with a toothbrush or peel potatoes in the galley. We hated doing anything in the galley.

Later on, I graduated to "security watch," which meant I patrolled the whole ship. I prowled around all over it to make sure everything was in order. That was much better than just the port side deck.

Another one of my duties was to keep the captain posted of our stats. When the captain went to sleep, he knew the route and speed of the ship. If any of that changed, which it did (Often, the changes were planned ahead of time.), the officer would say to me, "Notify the captain that the ship changed course at *such and such* time, and is traveling at *such and such* knots."

I hated to knock on the captain's door. He slept so lightly, you could just barely knock, and he would answer, "Yes." He already knew we were going to change course and knots, but he had to be told, anyway. I guess he just wanted to make sure we did it.

27
Coming Home

t was the fall of 1954, and my four-year commitment to the Navy would be paid up on January 5, 1955. There were eight others on the ship who would also be coming up for re-enlistment in the early part of January, and the Navy gave us all a choice. If we were not going to re-enlist, we could go on home early for the holidays. If we were re-enlisting, we would just stay on. Not one of the nine chose to stay.

I have always said that if it was just about me, it would be easy to "defend my country." But I knew that every choice I made would affect my mom, my dad, my brother, my sisters, all my other relatives, and on, and on. I didn't want to add any hardship or worry to their lives if I didn't have to, so I headed home as quickly as I could.

I would have been discharged on Monday, November 22, but they found a spot on my x-ray, so I had to stay one more day. Then, on Tuesday the 23rd, I got a doctor's release and a ride home with Felix Fisher and his wife. Felix was from Coweta, and I had worked with him on the ship, so we knew each other pretty well. He waited for me that extra day, even though he could have gone home on Monday. We drove forty-eight hours straight through, taking turns driving, and they dropped me off at Margaret's house on Kershaw drive. I rode on home with Margaret and her husband for Thanksgiving dinner, November 25, 1954.

Looking back, I am convinced that Thanksgiving Day was the perfect day to come home. What better day is there to be ending one career and starting another phase of life? I was grateful for the years spent in the Navy, and excited about what I would do with the rest of my life. And right in the middle, between the past and the future, was "home." Driving in, the old farm looked like a "long lost friend." I was coming home.

28

Getting Hitched

I came home, but everything was different. My mom said Dad lost interest in farming when I left for the Navy. The year I came back from the service, 1954, my dad had taken a job in town at the ax handle factory and leased his land out to a neighbor and a good friend of ours, Walter Coppin. Walter was still trying to keep farming, but he didn't last much longer, either. I think he farmed two more years after Dad quit.

Most of the small farmers quit trying to farm in about 1954 through 1956. Some of them might have lasted till about 1960, but for the most part, the life that we knew before WWII was gone. Everything changed. The small farms pretty much disappeared and went to pasture and cattle, as we use the land today.

As soon as the dust settled from my trip home, I made a bee-line to see Betty Jean. I first met Betty when she was about fifteen. But I was twenty, so I didn't pay much attention to her at the time. Then, in 1953, I came in on leave and stopped to see Margaret at her house in town. I noticed Betty, who was seventeen years old by then, hanging out clothes on a clothes line in her back yard.

I thought she was the most beautiful girl I had ever seen. I asked Margaret about her, and she said, "You know her! That's Betty Jean Harrison!"

I went right over and introduced myself. At that time, I lacked about a year being discharged from the Navy, so we decided to write each other while I was gone. When I came home, we started seeing each other again.

Then, after a couple of months, I took Betty Jean out driving around for her birthday, and I gave her an engagement ring. One week later, on February 12, 1955, we were married. I was twenty-four and she was nineteen when my brother-in-law, Tom Greene, married us at Betty's house.

We can't agree, now, on whose idea it was to get married so soon after our engagement. I say it was Betty Jean's, and she says it was mine! All I know is it must have been a *good* idea because we're still married more than fifty years later.

Betty Jean and I on our wedding day, February 12, 1955.

29

The Bottom Line

As we neared the end of the 20th century, Tom Brokaw wrote a book called <u>The Greatest Generation</u>. That "greatest generation" he talked about in his book was people like my dad, my older brother, and two older sisters. They were the people born from about 1900, even a little bit before that, until about 1925 or 1926, who lived through the Great Depression.

I agree with Tom Brokaw. That truly was the greatest generation that ever lived on the face of the earth up to this time. There was just so much hardship they went through that other people probably never will experience. I didn't have it very easy, but I didn't have it as rough as they did. They were truly the greatest generation of this time.

I'm going to cut this a little bit short. I know I've only gone to about 1950. There's so much more family history we could go through, and we will, time permitting, and the Lord willing. My family tree would include my brother, Junior, and his children, Ronnie and Donna; my oldest sister, Louise, with her family, Gary, Dr. Judy, and Tommy; Margaret and her family, Rocky and Susie; our own Cary Lee; and Sally's family, Stanley and Rodney. One of these days, maybe I'll make a tape about some of the things we did with them and how they have blessed our lives.

I have truly had one of the greatest families (I don't know of any one of them that I'd ever trade) because I had the finest brother and three sisters that God ever put on this earth, and the greatest parents, of course, that ever lived.

This is my mom, Ruth Rains, age 8, standing next to Granny Moore, in 1911.

~A Tribute to My Mother~
A Woman of Virtue

My mother, Ruth, was born in 1903 and was adopted as a baby by William and Lily (Casteel) Goodwin. William was a vaudeville dancer, and traveled a lot. Lily passed away when my mother was only eighteen months old, but before Lily died, she asked her mother, "Granny Moore," to raise the baby. The Casteel family, Granny (Casteel) Moore and her sons, Thie and Joe, along with my mother, then moved into this area from Texas. This is where they raised my mother, Ruth. Mother's adoptive uncle, Joe, who married late in life and had no children of his own, was probably the only father figure my mother ever had. Granny Moore passed away soon after I was born, and that is when Mother found out that she was adopted.

The Casteel family lived east of us, and in 1936, when the drought hit Oklahoma, they decided to go to California. They heard they could make a dollar a day. That was pretty good money, so they moved to California. I don't know how they made it there, but they did.

They came back to our area "to stay," they said, but they

left again. This went on for years, but one summer, in 1943, they came back and moved into a log cabin on the government flood-control land. It had a dirt floor, one room, and logs with clay in the cracks to keep the wind out. It was on the Black Jack Ridge just north of where we live now. They were so poor, like everyone else, they didn't know which end came and which end went, but they were hard-working, honest people. Every evening, they would fry fish that they had caught, and we kids would slip over there whenever we could and eat with them. They loved to fish, and they were fun to be with.

But one day, the Casteel's decided it was time to go to California again. They left in a Dodge car with tires so bad, you could almost see the inner-tubes. There were nine people in this Dodge, plus a cook stove strapped on the back, and two or three mattresses tied on top. It was *loaded*.

They sent a letter back three months later saying they had made it to California. They told in the letter they had nine flats before they reached Checotah (about 25 miles from here). They ran out of money along the way and stopped in Arizona to work. When they earned enough money, they went on to California. This is the kind of people they were. They were never in a hurry, took things as they came, and rolled with the punches. They were true "Okies."

Thie and his wife, Nora, had eight kids (five boys and three girls). Their youngest daughter, Marie, was good friends with my sister Margaret. Not long after Margaret got married, Marie married a guy named Edgar Bales, and he became one of the best friends I ever had. In 1944, Thie died and was buried in California. Nora came back here to stay, then, and she and Marie are both buried over at the Elm Grove cemetery.

Joe had been a big influence on my mother and helped a lot with her. He stayed with us some when he was sick, till they wanted to go back to California. He made it back to California one last time, and was buried there along with his brother in '48 or '49.

This is just a summary of the people who took care of my mother and saw to it that she was raised. They did a good job, even though they had very little. I don't guess she ever lacked for anything, no more than any of the other kids at that time. Times were just hard on everybody, but she came through in fine condition. She was a beautiful person, and the people who raised her were good people.

Mother was known all around these parts for helping anyone who needed help. Whether nursing a sick neighbor back to health, sitting with their babies, cooking, sewing, you name it, she was glad to do it. All the neighbors knew my mother would help them out in any way she could. You kids, remember that. My mother was one of the finest people that ever set foot on this earth. She was straight A all the way.

Mama passed away October 26, 1981, and is buried in McLain cemetery right next to my dad.

My dad, Joy Rains (far right), with his parents and siblings.
He was 15 years old when this was taken in 1915.

~A Tribute to My Dad~
A Man of Integrity

My dad, Joy Rains, was one of the most successful men I ever knew. He was born January 28, 1900, the fourth child of Sally and Joed Rains.

Joed's family came in here from Missouri in 1890. Joed and his dad traveled here in a covered wagon, settled in the McLain area, and farmed. The Old Man Rains, my great-grandfather, and my grandfather, Joed, were big cotton farmers. They leased and rented all the land they could get their hands on in this area and grew cotton. Of course, back at that particular time, cotton was "king" because it was the cash crop. If you had a patch of cotton, you would get some money in the fall of the year. There was always a market for cotton.

Dad's mother, Sally, came here from Tennessee with her folks, the Holder family, not much later than the Rains people did. The Holders traveled through here on their way to Texas. They were going to settle in Texas, but they stopped along the way to help the Rains family pick cotton. Their daughter, Sally Holder, and my grandfather, Joed Rains, hit up a courtship, and she became my grandma. They had eight children. My dad was born in 1900, ten years after the Rains family settled in McLain.

When Sally and Joed married, the Holders decided to stay in this area, too. There's a lot of Holders still in this area around Warner, McLain, and Muskogee. They are all our second cousins and a bunch of fine people. We really have a good time visiting with them.

Joy Rains, my dad, was always a hero of mine. He was strong, stood six foot tall, and weighed 200 pounds. I remember when I was a youngster, I would crawl up in his lap, and I would play with his hands. They were so big, and they were so rough, and yet they were so... when you think about it... they were also tender. His hands were big, and I loved to play with his big fingers and look at them because they were scarred from a lot of hard work.

My dad had beliefs that were as strong as any man I've ever known. He was as honest as the day was long, and he instilled a lot of principles in his children. He put a lot of values in our lives, in our thoughts, and in our minds. We have always given Dad and Mom the credit for imparting to us the standards that we have used throughout our lives, and in whatever profession we chose.

I remember when I was a kid, Daddy and I were taking our team and wagon down the road, and I saw a brand new bucket lying in the ditch. It was a shiny metal five-gallon bucket that would have cost every bit of two dollars, which was a day's wages at the time. I said, "Stop, Dad, and I'll go back and get that bucket!"

He said, "Nope. Whoever lost it will be coming back to get it here in a few minutes."

That was his way. Respect other people's property. Don't take what isn't yours. Don't cheat anyone out of anything.

One of the things Dad always strived for, and worked hard for, and always dreamed about was "one day" his kids would have it better than he did. They might not have to work quite as hard as he did. I heard him mention several times that maybe "one day" we would not have to do *this*, or we would not have to do it this *way*. He wasn't really complaining. He just wanted us to have a better life and to have it a little easier to make a living than the way he had to do it. And he achieved that. That's why I said at the first he was one of the most successful men I ever knew, because he accomplished his dream for his children.

Joy Rains died May 10, 1976. He's buried over at McLain cemetery, along with all of his sisters and brothers. His mom and dad, his grandfather and grandmother, all of his uncles but one, two of his children, and two great-great-grandchildren are all at the McLain cemetery.

Epilogue

From where I sit, I can see a Dooley headed down the dirt road. I see a cloud of dust back west billowing up over a clump of trees where an old house used to sit. The Caroll family lived there. They were a good family. They had it rough, just like everybody else did. The three boys had to sleep in the barn so their sister could have the bedroom. But one of those boys, Art, joined the United States Air Force and retired as a Colonel.

The old Dooley's a long way east now, about a mile and a half, and the dust is boiling up over another place where a young man named Cardell Coppin was raised and still lives over there. God called him to preach, and he did. And because of his preaching, hundreds of lives in this community have been changed, including mine.

I can see the Old Home Place from here, and I can see out in the yard, for just a split second, a little brown haired girl named Kimberly (my great-niece) who lived there after we moved out. She wanted to go to school, and she did. And, oh, how proud she made all of us when she finished at the top of her class at the University of Oklahoma.

The dust is almost settled again, and for just a few minutes, I look back at the land where we moved fifty-some years ago. I don't expect anyone to ever love this old place like I do. The Lord gave it to me for a little while to watch and care for, and I have enjoyed it so much.

I just wonder as the years pass, and I look down from above, what will come off of that old dusty road in the next fifty years. As of right now, only God Himself knows for sure.

Afterward

The government now owns all but fifty acres of the old Pugh Place where we lived and farmed a hard living for five years. We had an opportunity several years ago to purchase those fifty acres, and we did. Some of that fifty-acre plot went to a great-granddaughter of Joy and Ruth Rains, Kimberly (Price) Allison, and her family. They moved down there and built a house, and there's six of Joy and Ruth's great-great-grandchildren now living on part of the land that my dad had farmed back in the 30s and 40s. It's quite a coincidence that those children are playing and roaming in the fields up and down the little creeks there, like I did when I was about their age or a little older. We're glad that one of the places Dad sharecropped has come back into our hands.

CPSIA information can be obtained at www.ICGtesting.com
Printed in the USA
LVOW07*2304270115

424625LV00002B/2/P